Renaissance Woman

Deéjah Rios

Presentation by *BookLeaf Publishing*

Web: www.bookleafpub.com

E-mail: info@bookleafpub.com

ISBN: 978-93-95314-78-7

First edition 2023

I dedicate this to my mom and pops. Thank you
for always giving me a safe space to be creative.

The Double Standard

I am not angry because I was born a woman and
he a man.
I am mad at the line that has been drawn
between us. Opposite sides view the
same line differently.
I was not sculpted out of clay and descended
from a god, nor was he- we
ascended from the same tunnel. The tunnel of
love had us ally against each
other, and we were demanded different things.
He- a god, and I at his mercy.
Same world- different battle.
He has never been asked when he was going to
learn to cook. He picked up a
fork with his mouth wide open and was fed the
world. As a woman, I am born
hungry. Hunger demands to be noticed, and
starvation is overtaken by
unfulfillment.
I was born with a predetermined title- If I were
not to fill that role, then where do I
stand in a man's world? I am not your daughter,
your sister, or your mother- I am
simply a woman. I am angry because I cannot
just be a woman, and he is just a
man.

The Star and her Moon

And so, they set aside their differences for one moment
and ignited the sky by fusing into each other.
The stars twinkled in applause; the world fell
silent, and love was all-consuming.

My Secret Garden

When I am mad at her
I claw at the ground to get rid of her.
I cannot get rid of her.
I wish not to.
I cry to bring her back.
She is already there, waiting for my tears to
nourish her.
I cannot get rid of her.
I wish not to.
I de-root native species to make room for her.
I did not want to get rid of her
So I made space for her.

I was half bloomed when I met her-
A small bud in a concrete jungle.

She is a survivor -
She blooms in the concrete.
When I ground myself
I tangle my roots with hers
We are separate
We are one.

Message from the Divine Feminine

A woman's womb is immortal- And if she cannot carry life. She is still a woman.

Dear Friend,

Do not dip yourself in other peoples wax. You will not melt the same.

To: My First Heartbreak

I made a cameo once in a while in your life, but
to me, it was the main storyline.
You were as constant as the seasons in my life.
Natural, sometimes unbearable but desired in all
forms of it. I accepted your
Winter and loved the Warmth of your Summer.
Spring would have sprung, and
the cycle continued because I bloomed in your
springtime. I probably won't ever
stop writing about my first heartbreak. Because
the other winter heartbreaks
won't ever be as cold as the distance, you had
kept. Or the scorching Summers
that made me feel dry and begged for your thirst.
I've adapted and am now ready
for any season- no matter how unbearable or
tolerable it will be.
From: Your firstborn

A Songbird and her Empty Cage

He mistook my glances for love. But I did not
stare with adoration, only
confusion. Am I caging myself for him? When
he decided to part ways- I was
free, and he was holding the puzzle piece that
never fit in my puzzle board. He
did not realize he had tried opening a cage that
was already open. He assumed
he had the privilege and power to release me.
But I had flown away so long ago.
What a pretty cage- Decorated and gleaming
superficially- But hollow and empty
on the inside. No room to fly, only to showcase.
My mother raised me to be a
phoenix, But I felt like a muted songbird. There
is nothing wrong with being a
songbird- But I was not empowered in his
presence. I could not flap, nearly
flutter.

October Showers

The towel that held you longer than I did is still hanging on my bathroom door.

Messy Feelings

The kitchen's checkered tile floor sets the match.
It's you vs. me.
Or is it me vs. me?
I've spilled my sadness all over the floor, and
you mop it up and reuse the water
each time this happens.
What a mess I am. I climb up the walls, so you
can't see me- you take a seat,
pour a glass, and wait—blank slate shadowing
the checkered tiled floor with my
self-deprecating blabber—you look up. I look
down, and your patience soaks up
my mess. I climb down onto your lap, and I stare
at the little bit of sorrow
slithering toward your shoe. You squish it before
the fear starts flooding in, and
the mess is bearable again.

Womban

She immortalized me- for I am the poet that
speaks from her.

The Witch and the Monster

Some days I tell myself I am Scylla- most days,
I am Circe... a misunderstood
witch not reaching her full potential yet. Can a
lost soul and a monstrous one
see eye to eye, or are they the same?

The Pact

When he picked me up, I opened with no
hesitation for him
I shared intimate details with him, I saw him
through his phases.

Without saying a word, he understood every
inch of my brain-
When you read me, I want you to dissect me.

Outside my pages, I hate to be perceived

But between these layers of pages-
You can be as brutal to me as you are with
yourself.

Take it out on my poetry and feel what you feel.

You can hate me, or you can love me-
Sometimes feel indifferent

that's okay
I want it to be just between you and me

You can whisper your secrets, and we can make
a pact-
You can yell at me.

Hell- toss me across the floor.
You'll pick me up again, and we'll reminisce on
our time together
I'll be here
With the same old story
Go and live your life but
pick me up again, and we can talk about what
we missed.

Old News,New News

My tears filled up the bathtub
Not washing away my sadness but soaking it in
That's when I knew I couldn't swim away from it
I'd have to unplug the drain and dry myself up
I don't wish to drown- that'd be too easy

I just wanted to be swallowed whole into the
drain and escape into the ocean-
If I were ever to make it there, I'd lie on the
bottom of the ocean floor and take a

nap.

The Fools breeze

He sought sanctuary in her smile
Her childlike wonder enthralled him
She was a breeze that left a warm scent, and he
trailed right behind to feel her
warmth.
She is just passing through a flower would
declare to the fool
He did not listen- nor did he care
She glowed, and he always would seek comfort
in the warmest of places.
I am the cold in need of your heat, the fool said.
I am the heat in a condition of your heart, she
replied with a smirk.

Daily News

You have taken over every thought of mine- that
you have become the headline
of my daily newspaper.
War will always be around, and the stock market
might crash often, but you are
right on the first page that I want to read every
morning with my coffee.

Renaissance Woman

If I allow my world to crumble-
Will I enable the rebirth that comes with it?

That plague over takes my inner workings
When will I discover my renaissance?
The destruction is my own doing, but the
rebuilding will be historical.

Bruised Petal

18

The world suffers and she suffers with it.
Her petals are bruised but she blooms beautifully
in the violet hour.

Greek Fantasy

It was the smell of nectarines lingering in the air
while we rooted into each other-
if we had grown into each other, we would've
discovered a new species of fruit.

The cotton candy sky illuminates off the soft
waves. Your tan skin- golden from
the Summer sun- my appetite is insatiable. I am
drawn to licking your sweat as
you lick me as if I am ripe and ready for your
consumption. Oh, to be consumed
by you-swallow me whole and I am yours for
the taking.

The Snowstorm

When I defrost myself from my coldness, will I
seek warmth at someone else
campfire? I've wandered aimlessly in the
snowstorm.
I was not prepared- dressed for Spring but still
bearing my frostbite.
The storm starts to settle, and I seek out
firewood.

Goodbye Concrete Jungle

She sat quietly on the mushroom bed. Her violet
hair cascaded over the
matching colored fungus. Her reflection through
the raindrops becomes distorted
when the fireflies come out of the woodwork to
play. Singing frogs and an
orchestra of crickets are displaying a song. A
centipede with red ballet shoes
walks by, and happiness arises in her chest- the
concrete jungle is just as noisy
but simply does not compare to the home of
mother nature.

The Mermaid in the Bottle

The mermaid in the bottle was a destination
point for sailors.
Some passed by and stared at her with sympathy
and awe of her beauty.
Some would holler and try to break her glass
bottle- no luck. Their ships would
sink faster than the sunset and be left to deal
with the devil himself.
Others with wisdom would talk to her and feed
her- for she would return the favor
of company and food by giving any coordinate
the Captain desired. She had the
map of knowledge and knew where every single
point was.
Questions stretched across the seven seas about
the mermaid in the glass
bottle.
It was a curse that could not be broken. She
waits a millennium- in that time, she
meets heroes and monsters, and not one has ever
asked her where she would
like to visit.